Pretempathy by Gemma Darbon

CW00822367

Pretempathy

2023 Amazon Kindle Direct Publishing

by Gemma Darbon

Also by this Author:

The Key to the Enigma: Unlocking our Poetic Potential

2018 Amazon Kindle Direct Publishing

A Psychotic Influence- Poems of a Psychotic Journey

By Gemma Darbon

2011 Published by AuthorHouse

Dear Joe

Thank you for your kindness, your honesty, and your faith in God - keep on doing His work.

Gemma -x-

God bless you

Pretempathy

-By-

Gemma Darbon

Pretempathy

This book is dedicated to Rebekah Rose.

I am just so grateful that we are sisters.

I am so, so proud of you.

Thank you. For everything.

This book is also dedicated to Roxana,

My True Far Away Friend from Romania.

I am ever so thankful that we met.

I couldn't wish to find a more brilliant

Inspiration to me than you.

Foreword

In the meantime; a break from the excessive routine of staying static in a constantly-shifting world, I pick up my phone, within the eye of the psychological storm of Post-Traumatic Stress Disorder, and I begin to write...

This book is for everybody who has ever felt like nobody.

For anyone who has to stay awake just so they never have to wake up to face another day of their battle (it is not another day, without a rest in-between; just within the same timeframe measurement, seemingly).

For anyone left in desperation, to the point where they are not accountable to make their own decisions.

This book is for anyone who understands mental illness and struggling with either low mood, fear, delusion, or constant, seemingly never-ending struggles with guilt, shame, hyperactivity, dieting to extreme or binge-eating-

 however you cope:

Because "There is light at that end of the tunnel,", or so they say... I really do not appreciate this cliché, either.

This book is also for people who care about the above, along with topics regarding this sector of the general public, the system behind it, and a first-hand account of experiencing this... from the inside.

I have been hospitalised for 29 psychiatric admissions, so I must've done a few things wrong along the way (understatement), and yes, so have the system, which although meant to treat, doesn't always treat with correct treatment, and it is a shame, because it not only wastes human lives, but also funding from taxpayers' monies, and the lives of the service user's loved ones, who have to carry on without the brother, sister, mother, father, daughter or son who they have lost to the system.

Every action has its' consequences.

This book depicts every consequence of many of my own actions, and inactions, as it is important to me that I am the one to blame, because with PTSD. If this, or any amount of responsibility is taken away from me, it could lead to a deterioration of my mental wellbeing, and an imminent relapse, as it is hugely disempowering to tell someone they are not worth blaming, or completely irresponsible.

All of the above is portrayed in poetic prose, as, generally, my optimal means of communication, is through poetry.

So. I sit back, and I grab a cup of tea and a biscuit- care to join me(???), as I divulge the innermost workings of a troubled mind, hosting a little tea party for anyone who has ever acted out and found it funny when staff do not seem amused, for anyone who has just looked at someone else, and seen the similar level of complex instability in their mind, as is in yours, and you smile and so do they... and for anyone who hates themselves so much that they judge themselves (or portray themselves to others) as having only the pretence of empathy; or Pretempathy.

a cup of tea and a biscuit

Contents

Yet Another Day, Yet Another Page

An entrance leading to potential opportunities and the burdens of encounters more close,

Then through the door of overlap.. into literacy.

(Supposedly) .

Those eyes. Those gazes;

Snapping at my ankles

(Amongst the pre-printed, bound, gathered consecutive pages),

Attacking my practical means

And abilities.

The pallor...

The sheen...

I vacantly stare back;

Irreversibly unclean.

It's of no matter:

Snap away.

Leave me in decay here;

A decay which is Never-ending-and daily.

Yet another day.

Then it's time to-

Go away (from them to me)

As we unanimously breathe

A sigh of relief,

No more hearing the mumblings of the more fortunate,

Nor the contemptuous glares,

As they grit their teeth.

A breather for a bit...

I am no and more the wiser

In literacy, and almost illegible;

"I see,", they say, strategically,

Depicting no additional surplus to the usual amount of terror boxed-away within me.

Less fuss,

That way.

Yet another day,

Yet another page. Here.

Free From Reality

Alone amidst the chaos and the dwindling echoes,

A wave of melancholia envelopes me, and in seclusion;
I have lost all sight of my surroundings.

Only this: I am lost; and I have lost my all.

I know I no longer exist as once I did.

It had to be done deliberately: I am not running from
responsibility- not from an exterior perspective, at least,
as all appears to be well. "No broken parts... well, not
that we can see!". Shhh!

So it has quietened down now, and I reach for my orb of
information that is not just from others- but it comes from
me.

It pours out of me- goodness knows what is done with
whatever my piece is, and sadly, no longer a remaining
chess piece in sight (I'm so used to being played), and I
am wasted. No survivors left, and the darkness
encompasses all as I am here...

When the imminent darkness arrives to encompass it
all, just as I am sat here, I wait for the next wave of
nausea to arrive, just so it can pass again...

I am friends with my fears: the clock's rightful tick:

Ever-present, as always, and as we are continuing to
travel without moving, we still orbit, even subconsciously

-and once again, still trying; immediately, I gravitate towards the most intelligent person in the room...

(but the room is bare and empty.)

They have extinguished themselves free, and they deserve this freedom- let them go: there will always be another chance...

I am nearly alone, but never entirely released to be free... from reality.

An Outline

I designed

An outline

On the ground

Where I was meant to be

Drawn to. By me.

No trace,

No more,

Is all it was for.

Ignore the truth

(Or your eyes will get sore).

All you knew

All you were taught

Mind over matter

Isn't going to matter, not anymore.

All you can eat- it's food for thought- and I'm getting fatter

They'll have to make the outline bigger: I'm too big to fill their shoes.

Everytime I jumped

When things were broadcast on the news.

Not related to me

(only my egocentricity).

Yet still, so confused, about how much that I did wrong;

Where I was never prepared,

By being aware that I was capable of doing so.

But there's no turning back,

Not now, remorse is useless,

If of something as permanent as I am back here for.

They say that we are never here that long-

But when a day feels like a decade, and a year feels

So much more,

You begin to wonder why goodness is ever here,

Just to keep fighting for

- Now, you can't ignore that,

Because this ignorance comes at a cost.

It is never just one life lost.

Lost, tossed, left and cast aside.

Disguised ideals and those times we lied and repeatedly denied the truth until we turned away from the view of everyone, safely.

They come and we're gone.

Its like a donkey, with the carrot Just out of reach

(but too much in view),

Is there is no way they can

help us?

"There is nothing we can do."

Not a clue... and no idea.

Left wondering upon,

Misfortunate in life's giving- along with fear...

If we're gone, or anyone;

It is always for a reason.

This will pass and never last.ed.

Before she even realised

Her life has been irretrievable; gone too fast.

(She wasn't believable... on time).

It's such a contradiction:

How does one common wrong creating so many rites be fine?

Except, only if it didn't happen

Over and over at night.

It's the sort of thing we pretend only happens in the news, or to other people whom we never even knew, and who do not have diseases from which to recover from.

It's not an illness: it's their lives, so they didn't deserve this wrong

- but *we*?

Even if unseen; unheard about:

Disbelieved and we go ignored.

It still has happened, behind each of those closed doors.

And even I'm just known for a disorder or a few, as for still trying or wanting to be causing this all to come to an end...

Maybe, just to make an end of a time,

Where no consequences is a lie?

Too much in-built guilt internalised I cannot bear the eyes of the watching passers by.

So onto preserving the lives of those others-

They appear so much more in need (truthfully; they deserve it, and I, obviously, do not),

This might well lead to a purer scene- in time they would have forgotten me.

So, instead of plaguing all the clean, the healthy and the ideal; the evergreen: like a parasitical disease, that is enviously so much greener.

All seemingly, because

I need not to be.

The Short Skirt Says it All

The short skirt says it all

It's what is surrounding the idea-

Or even the notion of

...or am I imaging this?

It's that similar shame spiral

Going round in circles:

Attention-seeker.

To mention just a few reasons-

Of even rationale,

Of how a mind is power

And the stance says it is.

Play up to them and what they like. To become; to be wanted

But it's just not to feel.

Of having overly emotional connections;

Too powerful to break down,

and,

Synchronised within second-

Seconds later than

An affection or a liking to

Power.

Then... hours of talking into the night. Laughter with is better than feeling better then

Not if, but the unspoken about concept of when:

Of imagined connection

Between the line.

Nothing happened except

Expecting the worse

(Better off for better or worse.)

This curse wrapped around me.

That *oozing* with confidence isn't a good look.

Of mindlessly looking like anything that I'm not.

Just for a moment...

I forgot...

When all was not lost.

Only *You* Will Understand This

Every day that my synaptic pathways grew,

I wanted to be more and more like you

You were my inspiration

I wanted to do my upmost to do all that I could do

To help other people

To make others smile

It gave me a reason

That you got to know God

Made you who you are today

That you taught your view

You succeeded

You achieved

You could light up a room full of people to gain optimal interest

To propose yet another briefly drafted, yet deeply thought out idea

Who knew I would wind up here

-and not so charismatic and intelligent like you

I'm sorry for the disappointment

For the loss and the cost.

For the disruption for the heaviness and for the withdrawal and for the neediness,

The need for a life almost lost.

The need for greed

The need to become

Anything but the natural me

Born beautiful

Died ugly

Thinking of the example you set

Everyone you met

Was mildly impressed to say the least

You are not easy to forget

Even I haven't yet

The expectations that were given;

I have never met.

This; anyone could get,

If they were well-above average IQ

Intellect

We met in our minds

I aspired and dreamt because of you

But I soon leave you behind

-and I have to,

Even if I have changed my mind.

I levelled up too fast

None of us should be here last

In this predicament

I never meant for this to happen

-and I'm sorry.

I'm sorry

For the worry

For the sadness and the sorrow

Of not knowing if I will still be here tomorrow

For the morbidity, the self-pity

And for being a "Poor little victim"

Oh, poor me.

Me. Me. Me.

Needlessly.

Loudly.

Stupidly.

I'm also sorry for my negativity

-and for everything bad that happened to me, and because of me.

I got lost in all of this.

But I learnt that:

Actions have consequences.

My responsibility

I ruined my life. My body.

Everybody who I cared about

-and I plead Guilty.

I will miss you,

After. I hope I get to see you again, one day,

But I have a very bad price to pay to get to where you will go. And I don't want you to go.

Your home is with your family

As well as with God.

"You Are Still In There... Somewhere."

"You Are Still In There... Somewhere.",

She tried her best to reassure me

- Even though she was worried and scared inside.

So we all go through this dieting phase as teenagers: eating more, or eating less,

Don't we?

It's just a phase... Maybe.

Sometimes we feel affected by others and compete.

It was like a game, almost, to me; an addictive game in which you cheat

(Death)

To survive, whilst you try not to eat.

Some people do not move on, never move on... or not until a wake up call, where it's almost- or completely- too late.

They decide: it was their own doing.

We tried to warn them. They're an adult- and we couldn't stop them: it's their mind. They won't be happy. They never are, just obsessed over a number, a weight, a shape or a size. It regularly causes people to die.

She almost acted like she began to hate

Her own sister, in order to save her life...

What else could she do?

She shouted, she cried and she tried

To ignore it, before, for ages.

She joked and laughed about it,

Teased and mocked with wit.

A mickey-take:

Making fun.

She also refused to be seen with me,

It would have affected her popularity,

Otherwise.

She forced her own smiles.

Even *she* struggled, but where was normality,

For her, when she was growing up?

Her sister, and I took this away,

The very worst day.

The worst day of her life

I am responsible for this.

It was caused by her own sister; me alone.

But they're grown: it was their own decision. We were heard but ignored. We tried our best. There

was nothing more we could do... was there? We couldn't even rest at night; tormented, due to my sister's spite. But we seldom complain. She self-sabotages (she is still so full of self-hate).

A long wait. Debating with the idea to hurt;

I was on a mission- and a mission to disappear.

To harm what was left of me, that wasn't really.

Clearly, I didn't want to be here.

I almost got my wish... I admit I was so selfish.

It was meant to be to destroy me, deliberately,

But the problem was that it hurt others and not just Me. Me. Me.

That was the shallowest and saddest part, that broke my heart in two; divided into too many pieces, was the ultimate outcome, that was for my lifetime and the only future that I could see... followed by a torment in eternity could be why I thought

I deserved it

I deserved every minute.

Every minute- always under attack...

From myself; their sister;

their own parents' daughter.

She wasn't quite all-there.

"You are still in there somewhere."

She tried to coax me back, away from the water,

Patiently, they all tried so hard and hid their fear, but I was too far gone to be anywhere near

A window of time had elapsed...

But it wasn't enough; I should have known better at this standing point here.

So I'm standing alone at the end of a pier, burning bridges; saying goodbye to my old life... and how other people can live, be rich, be successful, be a mother and a wife- I just have no idea?!

Watching faces fly past me, lost memories. I try to hold on to be here.

Flashbacks.

Disorientation.

Surreal memories: so crystal clear... the hidden Gem,

Then the memories go again and I am now lost.

Mind detachment takes away the physical pain.

The time I meant it, so I didn't have to do it again.

Now my body is broken into a wreck and decay. I cannot do very much anymore. Prolonged pain.

I pay the price, everyday, whatever this has to cost.

I survived, and for as long as I try...

(To make it up to her; up to all my family).

I wouldn't be here, if I wasn't meant to be.

And it's now this way for life.

Chanced

I brush my hair with my hand

You understand that

I'm portable.

Everywhere you go, I follow you. I stroll.

Seems destiny is how it works; that's how this circumstance have gotta rolling circumference.

Chanced. Even a lack of secrecy has got it's alluring element of control.

Lost and found: I didn't hang around for long... and it has still taken it's toll.

Divide and diminish from the start until the finish. Layers spread and stretched more thin and a howling from within. No temper more to fly. I was watched as I flatlined here, and there is no escape for me: there's no override...

So, how long did it take to make me into this monster, or is this my mistake?

Even so I was made and create, But to create, though it cannot happen anymore.

Suddenly back in the aftermath,

in my former "On the verge-of-catatonia" state.

Now there's nothing less of me to hate.

Plenty more to regret.

Yet still I wait up weighted-up through my days.

To pay back my debts.

Why I have not given up just yet.

This is the Extent of God's Love

Our God who knows our pain, who heard our screams,

who heard our wails.

He wipes our tears away.

He will never turn away

from us

-for His love for us, it never fails. Those of us;

us who He has saved-

we will never demise,

as one new day,

after death itself, we will all up and rise, with

No more ill health.

A life of eternity; in God's paradise.

Our final breath is not the end.

Our souls make us each a whole, our minds:

they will mend;

Because God is our Lord, our Saviour, our comfort, our strength; our eternal friend.

He will shelter us from the storm.

He will keep us away from harm, enveloped in His arms,

He'll keep us safe and warm.

Beloved, our Lord, oh, blessed are Thee- Your love seeks out the lost, reaching out to infinity, Your forgiveness will make us free!

You are our only Holy creator; the only reason that I am me! You will rid us from the hurt put upon us. The cross was the ultimate cost:

The cost of Your only son's life;

He who You have sacrificed,

for us, so that we can also belong above.

This is the extent of God's Love.

Comfort

I wrap myself in spiked armour to confront the battles ahead -but inside I'm already dead.

Nothing is waiting ahead anymore for me.

I left behind my identity.

No good things are meant for me.

I'm lost in time: emptied my body and mind of what I look like on the outside- when this used to be of the upmost importance to me, but now I am an enemy, where I ruin, pierce and destroy all that was good, pure, or useful.

Immediately, inadequately, irreversibly, intrusively, and inconsequentially, I waste away, whilst intermittently wasting other people's irreplaceably precious lives: people who actually, for whatever reason, cared about me, yet, still, I push them away- it's to protect them from my recurrently mixing-up of past brutalities, forcibly not within my own past...but just a repressed memory. Besides, I was not built to last (it's not entirely disastrous, then, and nor a surprise, in their own or my own tainted eyes).

A disguised upward glance "Survival", they say. Survival of what? There's nothing left here to forget- and I just cannot... so, no recollection from the vast expanse within the disaster-led incompetence-trained brain between my ears: No level of empathy. No more fear. No more compassion- not here, not now, I've left behind years of starvation, and of has-been living on "rations", which is so cliché and of a typical fashion: the rational response of someone who has damaged themselves beyond repair- and with the greatest reluctance, I no longer care. The thought was there, and "it's the thought that counts", they say. Anyway, I wouldn't amount to anything: I'm even less today.

So fed up of not knowing now, that "no" was where I left off and not knowing where I left off and where to begin. That battle within: there's nothing more left to defend: I can't mend, so safer to end... to end up somewhere far and afield, now, or then, or when, to yield. I shield them from the ugly truth of harm.

Just pretend to hate them; to have wanted to make their lives a misery... "Such a pity," I smirk, sociopathically. Shirking away from any responsibility.

This is now the monstrosity that I am.

Calmly I walk away.

Something Happy

That was the moment I decided To give up giving up.

That was when I was living for

-Love-

So much more than just for me.

There was a lot a stake:

I needed to be here for my baby;

My little guy

(No best start to this life)

-And all it took was just to

Look into his beautiful eyes,

Cradle him in my arms,

With he; so tiny, but his grip on my finger was surprisingly Strong.

... He is the reason I had stayed strong, for this long, as well.

Suddenly: in a flash.

In a moment

-And all of this was now gone,

As I stared up at my plate from The bottom of my cell-

I realised:

"This is where I belong":

"The lowest of the low".

"Scum"...

I never realised how far wrong;

How far wrong that I could go

-But what a cop-out:

"Well, I didn't know".

HA! Well look what I've become

Now that I do.

This is so, so far-from just "Needing Someone to talk to",

(Couldn't you tell?

I didn't tell soon enough,).

As I'm proceeding to be silenced and here, henceforth, shut in.

That strength from within her; Well,

It didn't win.

Living off the state, living in sin.

To the point where I was unable to appoint a next of kin.

Disgust, distrust, and no more than pity

For a sad-act-sob-story- Identity.

At least, for the ones who Unfortunately,

Couldn't ignore me.

Now taxed-working persons,

+ GOV funds me, and gives

Me the time and the opportunity, To *Stares into the mirror*:

A waster of a Mother

A waster of a wife

A wasted life.

The gut-wrenching loss of Innocence, it winds me like

A stab-wound from a twisting knife.

I had my chances, and ran out of time.

I couldn't change.

Besides;

Too late, now, to decide otherwise, now with,

and without, my mind

(albeit divided),

This tactfully disguises exactly how hard I had tried.

I was not allowed to decide

(Shirking from responsibility; this, I cannot hide)

For way too long, led to my further ideation of suicide.

And even when I chose this to Override,

He forced her to "change her mind".

Her mind now gone...

Somewhere else, refined people

Sit in a different place,

Their view of sorts like me is like a disease

(and with great distaste).

They have not lived this,

- Have not fell from grace.

Actually is not an entirely misplaced

...Well, opinion.

However, it is me who is the one in the wrong.

However long it will take,

I am not aware.

The start of a new beginning

Where I try to care

About who needs me the most,

And more than ever before:

However long we were separated for-

This is the calling I cannot ignore. I said "No" more times than I am now saying "No more".

More difficult than I had imagined, but still a slim chance,

As I had to encompass him, them, again,

In my arms.

This time I would shield us three- and especially them,

From anything that is harm,

As the ability comes naturally.

This protective alarm-bell

To keep him safe and to get me well.

To make up for all the pain Caused to him.

To learn to accept, and to end that

To begin anew

This; the only thing as a Mum that I could do.

The bond which we have has the strength of empathy, love and truth in us, too.

And for his other brother, who,

He arrived at that point in our lives,

Gave me so many more reasons

I am determined from now on to make things right,

For their lives to flourish, and for all of us three, and for them to remember me, between the

Now more frequent times together that we finally have,

Gravitating together with natural Genetic affinity.

They are thriving; taking comfort in their own abilities,

The reality has dawned on me and them, and I will never neglect their safety

Ever again.

My Bikini Beach Body

My bikini beach body has old scars, cellulite and a podgy belly...

My bikini beach body will never be: faked, airbrushed, nor toned enough for the conventional mainstream TV.

My bikini beach body had been damaged and is disabled permanently,

But-

My bikini beach body is my own vessel that still, albeit painfully,

Somehow it carries me.

My body is my own and it is what I protect,

In order to extend whatever life expectancy,

That is still in me, as of what I have left...

It has also carried two babies:

I am the Mummy of the two

Best boys who I have ever met.

Thank you, my God, who created me, because:

My bikini beach body is no longer my motive.

I have to live

(Even though it is still so hard to forget)...

I'm just getting my life back,

Just for my family.

I want to be healthy, and to repay all of my debt.

I am not a bikini beach body: I will not conform to be that society expects.

I am not defined as a clinical number on the scale.

I am enough.

No: I am not an illness and my dignity will no longer be offered up...

For a free-for-all sale.

I am a human; diverse, curvaceous and unique-

and will not again inflict upon myself to suffer in silence, allowing my disappearing to communicate; instead of me needing to speak.

I am no longer unable to walk far; or to feel my legs or my feet.

My body will often fall down or become painfully weak.

But my body is now my own:

I AM allowed to be me- and-

My body is still alive (with my mind still in recovery...)

It is a new chance, every day, to start to live (to say: "Yes, I'm here to stay."):

Finally,

Because looking thin enough when wearing a bikini is definitely no longer my priority

When You Waited

I remembered you

You waited for me, almost all this time

-and you didn't miss a beat

You were suddenly there...

Yet again.

You were there for me:

When you visited,

When you waited.

Then I waited

Every week, patiently;

The best man I ever had

Happening to me

and I remembered *you*:

How you respected me

Surprises

When you'd arrive

And I saw your gorgeous smile

Every week, patiently

You gave me hope

We had a strategy

As there's an us seemingly

Happened seamlessly

Overnight, and my highlight

Every night a text,

Every week, patiently

Did I expect too much of you?

Did I take you for granted?

Did I lose sight of how much

You meant to me

(Uncertainty, now...)?

Every night, patiently

I wait for *you*, now

I'm sorry I've been a cow,

and not realised all that you do

For not just you, but for me.

Every day, patiently

I wait as you sleep.

I'm yours to keep:

Your very own pet.

I'm still here for my lifetime

I expect.

I expect too much,

Of you, of an *us*.

I must trust you.

Or all this distress; all this much fuss-

When really it is time

For me to improve,

For you to feel that I can

Regulate my own mood,

To not rely so much upon you,

To learn for myself to know what to do.

You opened your home to me to live in, too

And gave me a key

I still love you, Mickey (My Key);

I always will- and you are my rock;

You were always there.

I won't forget you,

How you waited

Every decade without certainty

-and suddenly you're back here with me

-and when you didn't miss a beat

-and I saw you again:

My heart skipped a beat.

Too many years apart,

You will always have my heart.

This is God's Love

Our God who knows our pain, who heard our screams,

who heard our wails.

He wipes our tears away.

He will never turn away

from us

-for His love for us, it never fails. Those of us;

us who He has saved-

we will never demise,

as one new day,

after death itself, we will all up and rise, with

No more ill health.

A life of eternity; in God's paradise.

Our final breath is not the end.

Our souls make us each a whole, our minds:

they will finally mend;

Because God is our Lord, our Saviour, our comfort, our strength; our eternal friend.

He will shelter us from the storm.

He will keep us away from harm,

Enveloped in His arms,

He'll keep us safe and warm.

Beloved, our Lord,

Oh, blessed are Thee-

Your love seeks out the lost;

Reaching out to infinity.

Your forgiveness will make us free.

You are our only Holy creator;

The only reason that I am me!

You will rid us from the hurt put upon us.

The cross was the ultimate cost:

The cost of Your only Son's life,

The cost that You sacrificed, for us,

So that we can also belong above.

This is God's Love.

Pretempathy by Gemma Darbon

My Godfather

He was the life and soul of the party,

His smile lit up the room.

He cared so deeply for others,

And he will always love you to the moon.

You may carry on his legacy,

You can strive to make him proud,

But every single success is lots more effort, because he's not around

He looks down on you from Heaven; he's watching from the clouds

And each of us who remember him, his smile makes more smiles all round.

He brought our family closer; he tried his very best,

He never wanted us to all fall out, I am assured, that we need to all have get-togethers,

Because all he wanted in his life was to love us all forever.

My (no longer) Lost Boys- by Mummy

Every waking moment, and even when I sleep,

Is missing you, wishing you would be mine again to keep

Everything wrong that I ever had to do

Is never anything that I would ever want to put you through

And that is why I walked away

My own worst day.

And oh how I wish that I could stay

You will never stop meaning the world to me

I love you forever until eternity.

Ziggy Cat

My very own laid-back Moshi-cat.

My cat,

He is so glossy;

The most beautiful of cats

(sorry, not to boast!);

Most purr-fact

in every single way

- his name is Ziggy

(Named after David Bowie).

My Ziggy, my cat:

He shares his life with me.

Ziggy has his two special black-and-white heart-shaped markings on the fur

on his body: This is the proof,

That shows why he was created,

Purposely

- In truth -

Created by God: this cat Ziggy,

he is living for love, and he

is living with me,

for his every future-living day.

I've had Ziggy, ever since

he was a little kitten,

by-the-way, you see,

- And he even chose me,

specifically

- I was smitten!

Anyhow now, currently,

Ziggy is two years old,

Living here safely, with me.

I've watched Ziggy grow,

so...

He's loyal to me, mostly,

Above all others,

I'm who Ziggy really loves:

He always just seems to know

However I'm feeling.

Ziggy is always right here for me

- whenever I may need him.

My Ziggy: he just knows,

seemingly, as understandably,

He just holds my hand

With his big fluffy,

Soft, white paw,

and he looks up at me;

All fluffy, cute and nice

-with such kindness in his eyes,

That he cannot be ignored...

and he just looks up, lovingly,

From sitting gracefully,

Right by me,

Here on the floor.

Ziggy is so graceful, agile

And elegant,

With gentle smile,

His happy-yellow eyes

- and he has his beautiful coat: Black as Night

(Black and White).

So glossy and silky.

Ziggy is so pristine,

With a huge fluffy chest

of white,

with white fluffy big paws

- as well as the white tip of his tail.

He also ensures that he's ever so clean:

Ziggy really is the best!

Ziggy is always there to help me,

His loyalty; it's without fail.

Ziggy's intentions are so pure

-He even looks like he smiles,

At me, as well-

Especially when he purrs!

Ziggy is ever so kind;

He's the best cat to ever

Happen to me- he always soothes my mind,

and I really love having him in my life.

Ziggy has a purpose:

He's here to reassure.

Actually, Ziggy

He won't ever ignore

Me and nor, anyone in need

(Apart from during his favourite times of day:

whilst sitting with his feed

- he exists best, for Sheeba

- he loves to eat!), anyway!

Ziggy: my fluffy-cushiony-cuddle-rug;

Splayed out for me here to snuggle right up:

This is trust and love.

Ziggy really understands humans

- He is incredibly clever.

He helps me make tea

and coffee,

As well as helps me at each meal... then, when praised,

He seemingly knows.

He stays there:

So cute. So fluffy.

I love this Ziggy forever.

I am like his best friend.

Ziggy also guards me at night:

He stays with me; endlessly.

Every time, without fail;

Watching me gently...

He helps me to get, somehow,

any kind of rest,

And as he patiently comforts me

I realise how Ziggy is the best.

Ziggy-cat: I'm so glad we met.

You have a personality,

And await, expectantly

For me to come home-

With the curl in his tail,

The twitch of his whiskers,

Nuzzling me, adorably.

I realise that he makes me

So, so happy,

Every time that I can be cuddly With my cat Ziggy.

Squiggly

A small and fluffy cat

Whispy white chest and white paws on

A soft and shiny coat of black.

So tentative; timidly placing his paws forward: one by one.

Sniffing around, searching for

New smells to find for fun.

So inquisitive, yet jumpy, and Fearful, as he seems

Almost always waiting to be

Captured and harmed by predating means

Always on edge

Terrified of loud noises

Fearful of sudden movements

And of the next move

(So we quieten our voices)

He watches his brother Ziggy

And copies what he does, too

Squiggles learns by watching:

The runt of the litter- and

The smaller of the two.

Very tiny once and even still so small,

But still growing bigger: growing fitter

(He also knows his name when it is called).

Squiggles is so nervous of noise

And flinches at any sudden sound

But his paws are still so dainty

And his head sniffs at the ground

He is very much

Surrounded by all of our love

Adorable, with his fur;

So soft and wispy to the touch

Squiggles' purrs are so seldom and so quietly, he almost
became a feral cat, but he has us now,

And he loves us very much.

Here and Now... Or Then

Lying on the threadbare floor.

I am wanting no more windows;

I'm only seeking for the door

(but the keys have left me restless...).

Scattered amidst the cause (and effect),

But it is no longer daylight; at least not just of yet.

There is no escape: Quick! Away, AWAY!-

Let's not speak of this matter today!

No more, no more!

It's time to ignore the past, because

It's hell to pay (well one day, it will be).

The convex mirror (I do not realise what I am looking at, anymore) in disgrace, as all applaud my forced disguise.

Any of my misfortunes gives another their fairer face *door slams*.

I just had to get believed on time, but it's too late for now. They didn't listen to me, or to the danger as my given warning... but how!? How?

I am not allowed, is my shirking away, as always, from responsibility.

Now ignored; they pity me with sympathy.

Formerly overestimated

Just one final sidelong glance, along with a sigh... they shrug yet again, and say "Lifer, goodbye.".

They all branch off one-by-one until I am left without a sky or a golden rising sun. Without it, there is no daylight and I am in fear,

As my loved ones grow away; further and further...

...Until only I am here.

All that matters to me is beyond what I deserve,

So I am left to serve the system for the rest of my years.

An echo in the darkness; a suppressed sob, as I realise that these are my own tears.

She Just Said Nothing

Life evades her, it dwindles into nothing

Memories simply fade to grey

And... gone.

She just sits there nodding her head:

She's fine, of course.

Smile, of course (at strategic points):

Look, live, try-

Don't fall: no-one will catch you,

Only concreate awaits, and there is no way out of this leap of faith (Enveloped in sadness; and still; she smiles!),

Still cowering by hate.

You cannot take back what happened,

You cannot make it go away.

Likened is this, is to the mediocre grey:

Grey carpet; frayed at the edges-I

But still safer than the bare ground...

So, she sits and she stays;

And still, she smiles.

I.Am. Nothing.

Nothing is all I will ever amount to; I'm not real.

Nothing is all that I will be able to feel.

Why hasn't the blatant sky fallen just yet-

Did he genuinely to himself, and others; swear to forget?

0

Nothing is all that awaits here for me.

Nothing is all to look forward to (at least, not that I can see).

Someday afflicted- and I am still not quite dead.

Do I need to repeat the question, just as of yet?

(Just like you did, but this time, it's me instead).

Nothing is all I can do to stop the suffering.

Nothing is all that will remain of me to bring.

Nothing is all that I've ever been.

Nothing will make this all go away.

Nothing is the only reason for me still to stay.

It always will be broken and forever I'm sorry.

A mind empty of matter to lessen the worry.

Nothing more is all that I can give.

Nothing is the reason that I still happen to live.

Her Control

Past Tormented Soul Destroyed.

She has power over me

Everything I say to her,

Has to be to her liking;

Her standards.

Her standards are high.

Then higher, even more.

With her at the top,

With the rest of us

Continuing to reassure her,

That everything she says

Is obviously what we would

All completely agree with.

That's how to live,

How we live.

Anyone who dares to

Step out of line,

Fails at everything else

In their lifetime,

Under her curse-

There's no cure for this,

And her dismissal

Ensures that all disregard

You also.... it's hard;

Hard to constantly be,

And have that

Emotional availability,

For her self-centred

Egotistical neurosis.

She is a narcissist

And anyone who tries

To value anything,

More worthwhile

Than herself:

Always needing to be

The centre of attention,

Not to mention the

Autonomously and carefully considerate appraisals,

Based on whatever she feels

Is the necessary light for her to be

Seen in... the whole atmosphere

Of the room alters, the minute

That she speaks.

She seeks and she craves;

Due to her own insecurity,

But forcibly casts her anger-

That she seemingly suppresses

-Very well-

In public places, in front of others; whilst she dresses to impress, which isn't abnormal,

Just petty, just small-

Minded. Why are we meant to care about her continual

Medical anecdotal remarks

And quotes?

Whoever sees through her,

Becomes her scapegoat.

And she will not let them go.

They will, firstly, become the Butt of all jokes. Spoken about

In her domineering condescending tone, only to laugh,
and get others to laugh as well, along with her, at the

Target's expense.

Tension arises. Arriving

Remarks become more bitter; more hard-hitting,

Degrading and belittling;

Looking down on them.

As she ever will, until...

She runs out of steam,

Falls asleep on the settee,

Whilst usually she claims

Not to sleep as much as she does, only because

She needs sympathy,

So she's predominantly

So tired, so weak, and

Everyone's own patient

And client.

As if we all need to know.

(We really don't need her

Discussing her imaginary

Diagnosis that she

Has invented, in order to

Prove that she is the MORE ill.

And if anything bad or illegal

Harm has ever happened-

To anyone she speaks with-

She decides it wasn't true,

And causes that person

To be devalidated, or exaggerate the majority- to rewrite history.

Murder mystery novels,

She never second-guesses

She knows all along.

Like she already knew everything that's going to go wrong.

It can't carry on... but it does- Until the day that I die-

Because I caused this to happen. With me being disgustingly me, my whole entirety of life. I stick in the knife. I take all the blame.

I embarrass her with guilt and with shame.

I endlessly create.

Manipulate.

Then we smile in the mirror;

And to the people we imagine we think we're beautiful to, in our delusion, in our head-

And imagined purity, beauty:

We smile.

To disguise our own hate.

(Note: This is how powerful delusion of persecution can be... and how ugly someone's mind set can become with this condition. This was during the most powerful delusion of persecution episode that I ever experienced, and it is not true, but pure delusion. It was the worst and the cruellest thing I had became).

Wider Issues

So, I happened to be nothing to them,

Yet we share same blood, same flesh, some shared experience, as Winter frost dries up those hearts of ice.

The mattered foggy mist of hatred blinds them.

Please, no more fights *she sighs*.

We cannot position ourselves on a nearby alliance anymore.

Guilty by a formation of an already-broken association.

Too much those parting words did hurt.

Too much they showered us in superior dirt.

Incomplete and never whole.

No inclusion, just prejudice.

Falling down a despairing black hole.

You cannot take it back; you cannot be united anymore.

Too many whispered-poisoned words.

They shun us out as they loudly shut the door...

(Do not believe everything that you've heard).

Truly Worthy

(A Song of Praise).

I can dream, in my mind

Shut out the world outside

Surroundings fade,

Into the night. I'm alright...nearly

(but, it's dark)

I can't scream, I can't fight

Nowhere to run away to tonight

In dismay, it's never day here...

Anymore. I'll be fine... but,

Within this troubled mind,

I can't go through this harm again.

Then, I pray a plea to Him:

"Lord; No more, no more!"

Suddenly, I don't look back

I do not brace myself

Pretempathy by Gemma Darbon

To be attacked

Suddenly I won't allow this,

To keep me in the darkness

Faith in change

Just to hope for another day

There must be another way

To find him in my heart and have believed the price He paid

To save our lives, to go to a better place;

a better place one day... for us.

Faith in love

Just to not give up

To let me know He's there, above,

This is what I can't explain,

But I just know, somehow,

Our Lord, He will reign... over us.

Faith in love

I am good enough

His love for us, is clarity,

I finally, know in my heart,

To Him.... we are, truly worthy.

Can't you see-

He loves you and me?

His love for us, in clarity,

I finally, know in my heart,

To Him... we are, truly worthy.

Faith in love

I am good enough

His love for us, in clarity,

I finally, know in my heart,

To Him... we are, truly worthy.

And to Him... we are, truly worthy.

Yes to Him... you are, truly worthy.

Through

I wanted to obliterate myself and destroy me.

I did not simply slip under- I was pulled with an unetheral malice;

As if a black hole had engulfed me from the inside out.

I was no longer aware of my whereabouts.

It was definitely not Heaven, there was no Holy Palace.

A scream that I heard that pierced the earth:

I did not realise; the scream came from me,

Until I saw everywhere: a sea of wires

Covering me. Constricting me.

I had not been aware.

Struggling and trying to pull them out: still screaming.

Screaming.

Suddenly, they were there: Doctors, and they told me immediately what had happened

(Their words almost washing over me).

"You're in Intensive Care. You've been in an induced coma.

Your Mum is there,

You had a heart attack and your heart was re-started

Do you understand?"

I suddenly didn't struggle or scream anymore.

This was not a place to shout...

... I looked around to see.

It was so dim and quiet;

Quite a peaceful yet surreal surrounding.

I found this forcedly grounding me.

12 beds here. All were silent, at rest.

Breathing apparatus working in sync.

Some of those people may never wake up.

Some who were not driven to the brink,

And nor did they deserve it.

Such sadness humbled me.

And there was sat my kind-hearted beautiful Mummy.

I was the one who had the good luck; luck rather than a pure blessing.

I did not deserve Heaven, which is why I did not go.

I cannot tell you how, because only God knows,

But I was given 4 chances... and every time I still woke up.

This shows that it was not my time.

This in itself emptied my mind of the pretentious neuroses

Of what I must look like on the outside.

I would walk away soon, only I leave the other 11 behind.

The Constriction of Anxiety

Will Not Win

You are locked in an imprisonwd mind:

Trapped inside.

Low in mood and confused

You feel like there's no future to Look

Forward to,

So only look behind

At what was

- and now that's all that I feel I could have been.

Unseen, I feel that all-too-familiar

Constriction of Anxiety

Pulling me in still

Tightening its grip on me.

If I don't move then I'm not in danger

So then it can't win.

I won't give into

It.

I must stay safe

Always so frightened

Pretempathy by Gemma Darbon

I can't imagine why,

But I'm still fighting.

I'm a good person

For doing this

In this prison of a body

Every single day

I hide under my covers

Undercover

Another night I cannot sleep

Lonely for another longest time

I prefer company of mine;

My own,

So I don't have to act like I'm fine

All of the time

I face outside of my own room

I cannot show them how I feel

My mood.

Its overwhelming.

Too scared to try

Because I am convinced I will fail.

I'd prefer no more failings.

So I do nothing at all.

Another Summer passed.

Now another Autumn or Fall.

To be locked inside

This mind,

It overrides my intellect,

And my capabilities

It's destroying what I felt

Was the best part of me.

Now I feel like I'm nobody...

Rationality contests:

But you are NOT.

I have not forgot all you have taught me,

For someone who so patiently

Helped me with my own studies

Intellect beyond her own years

Who has given up on hers

Due to The Constriction of Anxiety

And a very low mood.

When she doesn't see reality

That as a person, she is considerate, noble and good.

Never give up:

You are not all gone.

You are loved, and have a purpose here,

We've needed you, for this long

- and for so much longer.

You needn't not feel you are stronger than you realise

Your eyes are a window

To your beautiful soul

Here on Earth because

God made you.

You belong in our family

You have so much to give

You are a massive

Reason your sister

Has decided to try to live.

Your mind is not just Fast-working, but has wit and humour, too

Not to mention the compassion,

Empathy, and diplomacy:

This is the real you.

You have suppressed talents

and skills

Yes, living can be scary,

With limitations financially,

Would struggle to pay bills.

It must be so difficult

Feeling this stuck

Beyond what I could ever imagine

(but your cooking really sucks-

even better than mine!).

You are so beautiful in design.

You have so much

Knowledge,

Of so much in Politics,

Human Rights, and Policies,

Perfect manners:

You always say "please".

Intellect, also, in a rapid speed

Of cognition.

Your consideration and empathy

Are needed in this World

Your family are so proud of you

For being good,

For telling the truth

For using your wit,

Despite feeling s***.

For being you:

Truthfully irreplaceable,

- and highly capable, once

The Construction of Anxiety

Will Not Win.

Do not lose hope,

Do not give in.

You have a future

To be living in.

There is so much you could achieve and succeed at.

You are not alone,

And we are with you,

You are

Fighting

The Constriction of Anxiety

Will Not Win.

We all stand behind you

Rebsa -xxx

You Cannot be Writing That! #Seriously

When you realise we are all aging

Waiting our turns patiently to die

and you see only people crying for this, for the entertainment of the lie of youth. Of interests. Of beauty in tragedy and the glamorisation of this denial of time.

Time passes. Hour glasses fulfilling their grains of paths, gravity portrays their half-assed attempt of fasting and ever-lasting in a state of ketoacidosis, without ever seemingly, missing energy, carbs or satiety.

A satire of empathy; of disregarded communication-

So we tune into a different radio station.

Still desperate to sell our souls to the Nation.

National obesity epidemics are all on-trend; all the rage-

of a range of ever-growing figures of daily calories and fat consumed,

Roomier fabrics of a vanity size,

Under a disguised reduction of an integer, on a numberless label, sewn in as evidence (we have all been stitched up by this) as well as ass-isstive technology, which so many of us moreso rely upon.

On our lunch breaks we think we can make it a full hour skipping a midday meal, and then lapse in concentration, in better judgement, or in willpower.

This is still

A heavily secretive issue

That we cannot admit to.

... Because it isn't glamorous enough, like on the TV.

Nothing really to do other than deny we have an ED.

How to ruin your life in threefold

Loss of weight

Loss of bone density

Loss of life experience

Loss of health

Loss of wealth

Loss of the things you didn't acknowledge;

Of things you took for granted

- Instead you were enchanted by

A near skin and bone example

Of how a woman or a man or a trans should look

Of a gamin

Self-induced, yet an Invisibly-Processed Famine

With a nonchalant shrug

Of a shoulder blade

Razor sharp bones sticking out of skin thin,

The way society dictates

Cultural norms on weight

And the way anyone is insecure

About their appearance

Yet, this is what fuels it.

We are not to blame for shame-shaming.

Shaming the shamers is like

Hating the haters

Waiter, may I have a stick of celery please,

To go with my gateaux and potatoes?

The sort not to eat, just to look at?

That is how I imagine

First-World problems

To appear to be.

This Didn't Defeat Her

(I miss you, Benita)

She looked so beautiful, and always so very much in style,

But in a while, she would be gone.

She had endured too much, too long

(-and yet still she carried on).

She knew what she was doing, was the wrong assumption...

(But she looked like she did).

Hidden beneath her Latino tanned complexion, bright smile and enormous wide-eyes. Her vibrancy, and her bubbly personality- there lied her own harmed insecurity.

Always "Why me, why aren't I as good as who I was meant to be?", and needing reassurance.

There was mental instability, and fear and saddened damaging memories

(the memories that she gave up her life for).

She was affected, most definitely- yet, they ignored her final plea.

She was a beloved Mum and Daughter, and yet she felt too much pain.

Treated with disdain and laughed at:

This was exactly the attitude that fuelled her lack of life

Sadly, she died just to be believed; to prove she wasn't deceiving (and not to be unkind).

How dare they take away her mind?

She also left behind an eleven-year-old son

-and her perpetrator won.

Disbelief, stigma and accusations undone all of her own hard work:

Her battle with overcoming dieting and her disordered eating was difficult, alone,

But this didn't defeat her.

Crime did.

I miss you, Benita.

Goodbye, beautiful xxx

RIP Benita, my beloved and dearly missed friend. Taken into Heaven way too soon xxx

No Blank Slate

It starts out innocently;

Like a blank slate, I guess,

As then it moves into fast forward, before we get a chance to breathe

Before there was any chance to

Learn, grow, achieve

We didn't know-

We didn't realise,

As all of a sudden:

It's before our very eyes

The guilt, the hatred of ourselves; and of our lives:

Of every loss and sacrifice.

(Oh, and I'm tired of being nice).

We despise the times we trusted others, we feel there's no point:

No recovery.

A discovery of flaws emerge into view

(From their formerly submerged states),

They lied: all of the times that we were deceived with hate, but we believed them to be truth-

Yet we were falsely smiled to,

Reality was aware of who has gone to waste, for all this while.

I cannot run from this,

I cannot walk a mile.

And their reply is:

"There's nothing we can do."

"Because I Can"

"Why?",

I asked. I looked him in the eye, directly,

He turned to return my look.

"Because I can.". Was his reply.

He took not a second, as I saw The words fell from his tongue

-and at that very moment,

I knew he had won.

I was no-one to stand in his way

(aand nor was I allowed to have any say in the matter).

It doesn't really matter;

Well: not anymore.

Nothing

Ever happens

behind closed doors

("Yeah, sure.").

I was ignored-

and then there is

No more, to say,

-and anyway,

Night-time is only a

Day away

(and I am nowhere...).

My body will stay but my mind will be elsewhere and go away.

I will pay for that for years

To come (he's not done).

I'd begun to Give Up

On any idea -that anyone near could...

Assist me?

Strictly speaking, there was no Missing Link:

His ship has to float,

So mine had to sink.

I was on the brink of losing (never mind then)

It wasn't as if, it was if;

But more likely when.

Men aren't all like him, I think (uncertainly).

You see, I still have some faith In humanity.

Besides the point:

At points it was safer

Not to be

At all there, and for my mind to detach so I didn't have to care, and although I was no more scared than a wreck,

I still remember the pressure

Still then, on my neck.

But the real wrecked body:

It was just an empty shell.

I was hardened with armour

That so worn, wasn't well.

It was all very well

-I'm a sell-out-and-about

By now, so,

I gather myself together, and,

Whenever his memory springs

To mind,

My body repels it and I sit and rewind.

The torment was over,

Until it happens again

-but not at the time that

It happened,

This time...

Pretempathy by Gemma Darbon

Well, not exactly when.

Just me and

All of the rest of him and them.

Never mention those words that he said,

Because words like that

Hurt like shards twisting

Into the neck of the dead.

Those words' remains are still in my head,

Instead of happy memories. Temporarily, sure,

I can ignore it... for a while,

And I tilt my head, give good eye-contact and

Smile.

With hundreds of complaints

Already on file,

But.

"There's nothing we can do."

They don't suppose I am,

Of their view, being truthful,

Worthwhile, or of sound mind:

Too backward, too slow, and

Way-too-far behind by miles.

He did not touch me

Equals safety.

"Move along, there's nothing to see."

...And I'm not here anymore,

Well, not completely.

(His lies defeated me).

Because of Crime

Because of crime

I make myself stay inside

I can't unwind

Scared to close my eyes

Until any sign of morning light

Because I'm still terrified of every single night

Because of crime

Because of crime

Frightened; I cannot bear this fight.

Listless- have I finally yet again completely lost my mind?

Past memories never truly go, and trapped inside; they overflow

- Yet they cannot be accessed, and still, they rarely outwardly show...

Until I'm triggered, when once again.

"No"

The one word that I used, and not on its own

(But this, they already "know")

So then there's no stopping this:

Make it stop, "Please?", "No more."...

But no remorse. No sorrow.

Because it happened, as it will do; inside my mind

Forever scared of being harmed today, tomorrow,

Because of crime.

Because of crime

I have no life

I've lost now, despite how hard I have tried.

I'm tired- and it's no good- anyone else would not have deserved it... so why did I?

I cannot smile... not without feeling guilt and shame: it was not ever a game. Potentially, it's a systematic blame, and it has no name. I am not me anymore- I will never be the same.

There is nothing that can take away certain types of pain.

Because of crime.

Because of crime.

He took my life in his mind.

And then he won me as his selfish prize.

He disguised how much he loved every minute of my prolonged suffering.

My losses; my grief.

He fooled the whole lot of them.

Charmed them with his "pretemphathy", as he effortlessly lied through his teeth.

He was confidentially and fully aware (without a doubt), that I would never get believed.

I am crying inside, ashamed, full of pathetic self-pity, disgusted and repulsed at the injustice applied... and I just want to hide.

Because of crime.

If It Really DID Happen

If it really did happen,

Then why did that matter so much to me, to be
believed?

I wasn't trying to deceive anyone about that, at all:

It was to protect other people from what I had gone
through,

As opposed to trying to hurt anyone else...

I never meant to,

But we do all matter.

He had his reasons;

They both had their reasons to hurt me, as well as
hurting others

- Could be a strong possibility.

If I didn't get believed on time.

(Was only my belief, seemingly- what a cop-out)

They didn't know each other,

What could be the chance?

How conveniently played,

they may say to themselves.

But there was something about me that seemed to attract them.

Was it my vulnerability

(Which goes unseen, seemingly,

By so many)?

- Not that I wanted it to be seen, and maybe that is why.

I acted well, a touch.

However, we all gaze upon upon the very same sky. Never judge.

Some people go through so much, so young, that they have to see others hurting, because they are, and were, hurting so much. Hurting is all they know: They were not deserving of this hurt.

So a short skirt is trivial

In comparison.

Takes their mind away, of a fashion.

"Damaged goods", he called me

(Pot, kettle, black);

Is the worst (and unacceptable) comeback.

Emotionally,

He damaged me, but he was harmed so badly himself,

that he pretended to have

poor neurological health (When it was just poor acting skills).

Another man, again "Because I can" elsewhere, now,

His reply, when I had asked the other "Why?"

A man I felt love for, from when we first met

I saw the good in him.

We both had sinned.

I saw his mind in true colours

And we had each other

When we did begin,

It was amazing, in comparison.

For those times in our lives that we had been wronged.

So now and forever,

Our perfect dream; our "Wonderland".

But certain things begin

And behind closed doors,

Go unseen.

He was more clever.

More damage is done.

I did all I could to try to understand,

I was no such a man

Who was such a strong survivor

And he made me feel more alive than I'd ever felt with his wit, humour and attractively.

That man

He had him

Was all he had,

At one point too many.

He had his reasons.

As was our incompatibility.

Too one-sided.

I tried. He lied.

I believed him:

I was the bad one.

The bad Mum.

The blame game.

He came

Another night

I self-mutilated

I cried

I smiled, with fright

Then, he was alright,

Was his mind game

The closeness

The hugs

The intimacy

He stopped his drugs

I stopped eating

He took what he wanted

I lay there

I began to try to believe I did not care

He took what I could not give him

I felt guilty

He took

And so I gave in

I took it.

I took the pain.

I did not want this

I did not want to be

I didn't see

It wasn't humane

He hid it in well; was she questionably sane?

I was?

I wasn't sane enough...

And I hoped for this be true.

"There is nothing we can do"

Say those who tried to help me.

Exactly.

Why

There isn't

I put way too much trust and faith in the wrong people

And worshipped false idols

To look like them

Would be to not be me

So then I wouldn't be

Suffering like this.

Not allowed an opinion

He took it away from me.

Overshadowing me so effortlessly seemingly

But realistically

He knew exactly what to do

And how

And look at where I am now.

No mention of who needs me the most

I'm not there for them

So selfishly.

-and *they* truly needed me, innocently,

They needed me healthy.

Nobody believed me,

So I didn't believe me, either;

And decided that I must have been mad;

Mad to believe that I deserved respect

-and look who suffers the most

(Not me, unfortunately). Two inocents.

History repeats itself... but worse

If love is a blessing,

Then death is the curse.

The worst thing I could ever do. I hurt them (and it's not deliberate anymore

Nor was it ever, remember?).

As I sit here, I remember that I was lying on the floor (and so do they). Empty. Now. I cant handle the guilt. Gone away:

They are everything; my all.

I owe it to them to give to them a healthy Mum:

The fall that changed my life,

Just took time to kick in.

Back then it was like a game:

A game I didn't win..

"Because I can", he said.

Because I underfed myself.

And then I ended up undead, Instead of in his bed anymore.

Instead of in my own mind

Safe now: "No, not tonight".

It was always at night.

A Closed Door Within The Revolving-Door System

...and so you go it alone,

...and forced longevity

Whilst cohabiting peacefully

Within the revolving door system.

Alone amidst the chaos

Of a societal failing-to-keep -people-safe-kind-of -
approach;

Safe from themselves.

Safe from each other...

...and now safe from living

Another course of action.

Actions have consequences,

As a fractionally small percentage %

Of offenders do not repeat,

In comparison

Then never again cannot

Always be believable

Pretempathy by Gemma Darbon

Even if they don't.

So I suppose you'd get

My time;

Their lives.

Equals an exchange

Of services.

This saves Society

And the general public

It was an unwanted opportunity to no longer be

Within this category

Just... anon-person

Anonymously

She's back in seclusion again

Unseen

And another dragged again in for yet another fully-
clothed shower

Must have been hundreds of hours

To feel like they'd paid their price

Guilty.

That dead look within their eyes

Dead to anyone on the outside

But... once recovered enough

To leave the world of the secure

Sure enough,

Once you leave

You are not welcome.

Not welcome to study

Not welcome to work

Or earn

Or help

Or try

Or live

-and dying to escape this reality

Overwhelms you

It sets in.

They do not accept you

They do not want to employ you.

You are of no use

Pretempathy by Gemma Darbon

You are of no use

Clueless

And "normal" people

Will choose to assume this

Dismiss you, due to somewhat diminished responsibility

Supposedly this is meant to be let off lightly,

I'm sure. Ignorance.

From both parties.

Not able to part ways

From the burden of your shame

You remain

Dejected

But it feels again, like

You are not understood,

Accepted or respected,

Believed or useful

Good at anything

Rejected

Even things that you used to be good at

All you've studied

Gone

All your former life

Lived

Want it back?

Jog on.

Move along,

"You've done nothing wrong".

THERE IS, AND/ OR WILL

(Based on The Holy Bible Revelations... the first part)

There is no more

What for?

You sit there, waiting for closure,

But there is a broken door;

The very same door

That we were all warned about:

Half open, but will not close. There is nothing more than this

Awaiting for me, I know,

(And that's if I have

The best of luck).

There is no more?

Stop pretending:

It's never-ending,

So I am sending my

Best Regards

(And sincerest warnings)-

But the stars were taken,

And we will have no new mornings ever again.

Dawn never arrives, as the light has gone and we can't live on

As we try to end our lives...

But nothing happens.

There is no more:

What did I live my life for?

I destroyed what was made

With purity and love.

I damaged not just me,

But some others, you see.

Above love, is beyond help,

As it was just a pretence of Faith, I gave, and

Never good enough to believe in The Truth when it stares me, myself, in the face, in black and white.

I was created and there was no need to debate with hate as to Why,

As I cast my gaze upon the sky, Where it is beyond the Light, Where stars were taken,

And now, will be always night.

I may never be alright.

There is no more,

And still here on the Earth.

I never learnt to truly forgive: Could not even try to live

with that amount of guilt.

Where once, Earth was built,

It is now a whole black hole;

A pit with no beneath,

For all of the selfish,

And for how we lied through our teeth: But that matters not!

Do not despair:

He won't be there to Judge us anymore,

As we did not care,

When we acted like He wasn't there,

So now we can be forced to turn away from Him, and dwell and with all of the rrevelling in our own sin-

So falling, failing: we are forever stuck.

This must be why

I don't believe in luck.

-The End-

Useful Phone Numbers IN THE UK

If you have been affected by any materials in this book, or by anything and/ or, are struggling emotionally: please reach out for help.

You are here for a reason, albeit in your mind, if unbeknown to you. But you *do* matter. This is why you deserve the correct help you need, from professionals.

This phone call could save your life -xxx-

(All England/ UK-based, unless otherwise specified).

NHS (24/7)

(Choose OPTION 2 for mental health crisis open 24/7)

111

Or Emergency Services (24/7)

(for potentially life-threatening emergencies- Police, Ambulance or Fire Brigade) 999

Emergency Services (EU Wide 24/7) 112

The Samaritans 116 123

Shout (24/7 Crisis Texting Helpline Service)

text 'SHOUT' to 85258

BEAT Eating Disorders Adult Helpline 0808 801 0677

National Suicide Prevention Lifeline. 988

Afterword

Thank you so much for reading. Pretempathy, initially, was starting out to be designed for the people who can relate to my own personal experiences, people who are lost in the system; who have suffered injustice, and who feel like they have been in CHECKMATE for a rather long amount of time. Maybe for those of us, just... existing, day-to-day- instead of living. To those of you whom I have met along the way... and remembered: the people who have made me smile, despite their own struggles, and the people who I have made smile, as well, despite *my* own struggles.

This book is my perspective of the collective voice of the downtrodden, of those who live to boost others' morale, and this, in return, also helps them, as ultimately, these people are just living to help others have hope- it is their sense of purpose; a sense of duty they feel obliged to fulfil.

Also, for those who can relate; for those of us who may feel they have lost their identities; our initial sense of purpose. For those who understand what it is to have to live their life; to face up to the consequences, however harsh, of not only our own; but also others' actions, and look: you *are* still here- this is brave and commendable (well, in my opinion it is, anyway...).

This book has been written thanks to those whom I adore, as well as ultimately: thanks to those whom I harbour fear towards, and who I feel sadness for... and also because of, and/or *despite* of.

Acknowledgements

A massive, massive thank you, to all of you; the readers, for reading my third self-published book, that is within current circulation. I am ever so grateful to every last one of you for reading this: I couldn't keep writing without you reading, and without people such as yourself, nobody would want to understand mental illness. It takes empathy and patience to do so, along with trying not to judge: mental illness could happen to any one of us, at any given time... in various degrees of intensity or severity.

I suppose that I am in existence, somehow, thanks to those of you who spur me on. Primarily, my ultimates here are, of course:

My two most beautiful Sunbeams, my loves, my superstars. To my most brave and heroic boys, I love you to the Moon and Back: you are my world, and I am here because you are here because of me, so it is my responsibility to stay here for you boys, and to be here for you for as long as I can be, and as long as God allows me to be. You make me so proud of how you've flourished, and you spur me in everyday, so I can be here to see how your journeys continue. You are my sole reason I wake up every time I sleep, and why my heart beats. God created me, and blessed me with two miracles. You never cease to cheer Mummy up.

I am genuinely so grateful at how you both have grown up with seemingly endless imagination and creativity in your amazing and inquisitive minds. You have adapted and grown and thrived so well, for how insightful you are, how intelligent, empathetic, caring, adorable, funny and silly you actually are. I am so, so proud of you boys; proud of how far you've come, and of how brave you truly are. You have bright futures ahead of you two, to look forward to.

You are my entire world, as God is our universe xxx

This Book is Dedicated To

My lovely baby sister Rebekah Rose

I look up to you because you are ten inches taller than me! You are the bravest, wittiest and funniest woman I know- and nobody else gets our humour as much as we do.

Separated from birth, we were twins born 6 years apart, and before you were born... you were a sofa. Only you should get the credit for this, honestly.

You truly have the upmost empathy, diplomacy, a calming nature, compassion and understanding beyond not only your years, but also far beyond any amount that my patience, tolerance and extensive training could ever permit me to possess. You also have such wisdom beyond your years, along with your amazing bi-lingual Portuguese and English skills. You have such politically ethical morals, an extremely fast speed of cognition: such a high level of intellect, which I know you doubt... but you are the only person who has ever doubted you: we have not doubted your abilities.

You are so humble, for someone so blessed with ability and cursed with self-doubt.

You are a strikingly beautiful waif-like, tall, willowy, pale, elegant and Parisian. You have so much to give, much more even than looks.

Sincerely, I am eternally grateful for your forgiveness: forgiveness when no amount of apology will ever be acceptable for all you have endured. I could never have imagined my actions having so much effect on you or the others in our family. You are such an amazingly compassionate individual, with Perfectionistic tendencies toward yourself, yet you are so non-judgemental, patient and wise.

I wouldn't be here without you in my life. You are my favourite sister, apart from Sarah, and Sarah is my favourite sister, apart from you.

(Beard)

"Faith Over Fear" and God has blessed me with such a lovely family, whom are all very honest, respectful, polite, humble and brave.

I couldn't have written this without you in my life.

You mean so much to me, and you are very much loved, dearest Rebsa xxx

<u>This Book is Also Dedicated to My Dearest Roxana</u>

Dearest Roxx; my Far Away Friend... from Romania.

You are my dearest and most loyal of friends. For these last 13 years in knowing you, I feel so blessed to have you in my life. Your friendship means so much to me. You have taught me more in your second language than I could have learnt in my native tongue. Your incredibly high IQ, amazing communication skills, determination and driven nature, are all so important for your success, along with your discipline and perfectionism. You are also so intelligent, so beautiful, tri-lingual, such a caring individual, with amazing wit, lovely sense of style and fashion, along with great compassion and wisdom, way beyond your years. You are also an amazing Mom to your little girl, before all else.

Thank you for your patience with me... and for your only-ever kindness towards me, for your continued non-judgemental support... I am forever grateful, dear friend.

We met for a reason. God designed our meeting, and our friendship has only ever grown, as we have. You are my inspiration, and are worth so much more than you know.

Thank you for being you- and thank you for being in my life xxx

Further Acknowledgements Also Go To

To Sarah, My Sister

My really kind, silly, funny, determined and motivated beauty of a sister. You are an astute business-minded woman, a Mother, a creative craft lady, a Disney-and-90's-film-quotation-remastered-voice-actress (your very much hidden and often unused talent), and you are such a loyalist. I look up to you for how you've achieved so much, succeeded, and done so well, whilst setting such a sensible and level-headed good example. You're so beautiful, with your amazing eyes of Italian Royalty, your contageous humour and kindness- and plus you've got style (in the fashion of your attire, as well as your decor in your beautiful, grand abode).

Thank you for always still being my sister. I am so grateful, always. Thank you the most, for your forgiveness, too. You mean so, so much to me, and you are loved. I am proud of you for all you are achieving.

You are so strong and I love you so much,

Forever, Sarie xxx

To My Beautiful Mummy. Julie Ann

You are so amazingly determined, so funny, quirky, creative, artistic, and a very stylish woman, who follows her heart. You dreamt a life you always wanted, and you worked hard to succeed, and you got there. You have brilliant achievements and skills of professionalism, communication, advocacy, empathy, creativity with art and I am so proud of you for never quitting, despite everything. You are such an inspiration to me, for your consistent positivity and your incredibly kind heart, your generosity and your patience. You are much loved, and you make waves wherever you go. Thank you for your encouragement, for listening, and for your entire upbringing of us three (five now), instilling in us kindness, Christianity, manners, politeness, kindness, honesty, respect and patience. I love you forever, for all you have given of your life for us three girls.

Tbank you for your forgiveness, above all else, and for still associating with me. I've put you through worse than most Mothers could imagine.

You have saved my life on countless occasions.

I love you, always, my dearest Mummy xxx

To my Beloved Father Christopher

You never succumbed to anything that would ruin your family's chances to survive.

You are determined, and you put us first before anyone else, by working hard every single day in London, until you retired, bought a Jaguar, and, of course, an electric guitar! You are nobody else, other than somebody who will turn heads and raise eyebrows wherever you go, by making an impression with your very high intellect, your wit and humour that works on so many levels.

I would have loved to follow in your footsteps... and I could have done, potentially, had I not been so ill. You are someone I aspired to become like, and I failed. But I love you so much that I am honestly so proud of all of your success and your achievements.

Your years of success didn't come from nowhere, and fall upon your lap: they came to you from your extremely quick Mathematical numbers and English linguistic skills, your amazing photographic memory, your education and efforts in perfecting your work, and your attitude towards others, whom you could influence in a harmless and charismatic way. You can cause laughter and banter, by being an introvert who happens to portray as someone with an extraverted presentation; animated, influential, with good acting skills, as well, and you are my hero. Thank you for teaching me numbers and Christian values. You have instilled in us what we needed and so much more. One day, I hope to make you as proud of me, as I am of you.

I love you forever, my dearest Father xxx

My loving partner Mickey

You are amazingly handsome, and you become even moreso, with every day that passes with us still living together. You mean so very much to me, you are the most gentle man, and I'm so grateful for all the time you have waited for me. You mean so much to me, and I couldn't imagine a man better for me than you, not in my wildest dreams.... you are so incredibly funny, skilled, determined and knowledgeable, too, with your political views, Dungeons & Dragons, your Christian values, your outstanding physics and great mathematical skills..

I love your ginger hair, your smile and your hugs- as well as your cups of tea: you totally know the way to my heart!

Thank you for being here, and for my shelter, a loving home, for Ziggy and Squiggles our adorable cats, and for our hens (our rock chicks) xxx

A BIG thank you to Crosspath Care LTD,

Thanks to you, I have kept out of psychiatric hospitals for two long years. I am so grateful for how kind, compassionate, empathetic, empowering and professional your staff truly are, and I really like that you promote the independence of your service users, as this can create better life experiences and opportunities for very ill people, such as myself. I am so thankful that you offer me continuity of care, and person-centred care- with ongoing support, in order to prevent any relapse and further hospitalisation. You have helped me to turn my life around, and stay on track. You have helped me to gain confidence, and I am maintaining performing some tasks independently, now, that years ago, I was unable to do, including working. Thank you so much to your amazing staff. You are all so kind. The staff who I know, i get along with so well, and I appreciate all of your pro-empowerment ethics. Thank you x

Also To the NHS

A big thank you for putting up with me, for all of these 21 years under the mental health services, beginning in CAMHS (Child and Adolescent Mental Health Services), and the subsequent 29 psychiatric hospital admissions. Hence, I am alive today, thanks to you, as well as God had decided that I am meant to still be here, somehow.

You literally sometimes even had to treat me for episodes during my life, where I was unable and incapable of making my own decisions, and whilst I lacked capacity, for longer than my stints of being sectioned, I also was kept alive during the most critical times, by life support machines, thanks to the patient staff of Broomfield Hospital A&E Majors, ICU, and the treatment that has turned my life around, both in the former Vincent Square Clinic, Pimlico, and under EPUT, as well, which caused me to completely realign from, as noted by a Consultant Psychiatrist as "On the verge of catatonia". It was the most awful time of my life, following the four comas within 18 months of one-another...

Also, tanks to the wonderful former Doctors Chandralingham and Dr Williams and Bernie, of Collingwood Surgery, and also the amazing Dr Lita, Consultant.Psychistrist (thank you for your patience, understanding, empathy and empowerment),

Dearest sweet, lovely Kaylie

You are the sweetest, most kind-heated, non-judgemental and compassionate human. You have a contagious humour, an amazingly beautiful smile, and the brightest pretty sparkling turquoisest-blue eyes, too. You are so highly creative, incredibly empathetic, and artistic. You radiate positive energy and goodness into other peoples' lives, by doing good things for so many, without impatience. Thank you for never giving up on me, for your patience, your support- and for your continued appreciation and critique of my work.

You are the most compassionate to others, and you have so much empathy. One day, you will make an amazing therapist. You are an inspiration; as someone who has been there and decided to turn it around

You are **very** much loved and appreciated xxx

Dear C.

Your continued association with myself, has caused me only happiness and you are a lovely role-model and have brilliant-minded humour, patience, intellect, and especially honesty, respect and kindness; above all else. I really appreciate all your support over the years, and you are always such an inspiration to me. Always will be. You shine on others to brighten them up, with your compassio and your tolerance.

Much love xxx

Furthermore, to Bardwell. My D&D friends Richard, Hugh, Dan, Paul, Chris and of course, Michael!

Thank you for your non-judgemental and kind attitudes towards me, and for always accepting and including me. I appreciate this,

I adore role-playing with you all... the inn-jokes, and the ongoing banter.

You guys are absolutely epic, and I am grateful to know all of you. You Rock (and Roll, geddit?).

To all the rest of my family by Blood

My beautiful glamourous and witty Nan, Patricia, who is so positive, caring and vibrant. You are so brave, and so funny, so friendly, so determined and so kind. God bless you. I love you forever, Nan-x-

To Tony, Lia and Joe, Tara and Chris and Leslie, Rebecca, Lindz and Carol and Vince, Vicky and Dean,

Emma and El and Lee, Libby, Laura, Jen and Dean, and Mirra and Ian, and Aunty Nicola/ Nicowa and Sean.

I love you **all** very much, because that is what family are for. I know you don't all get along, and I hope to still be accepted by you. You are inspirational, my Aunts and Cuzs. Brave. Bold. Intellugent and a beautiful bunch of people. You all matter to me x

To those of us who are no longer with us, but whom are my loved ones, and in my heart

Grandfather ("Jim" was his Army Nickname). You were so respectful, considerate, Christian, strong and you courageously fought for our Country. You were devoted to my dearest Grandmother, and I would have loved to have known you for longer. You were incredibly determoned, witty and humorous as well as a skilled gardener and painter- even in your 80's!

My beloved Grandmother. A beautiful Lily, who was ever so humble, and instilled good Christian values in your children and grandchildren. You thought of yourself as a "plain Jane", but you were beautiful, quick-witted, determined, disciplined, well-mannered, well-dressed and so skilled at so much. You were amazing with us, your grandchildren, and I remember my every intetaction with you, with great fondness. You instilled so many ethics in me, that make me remember how respectful your generation was. You taught me so much, and I learnt from you even years afterwards, because your lessons were memorable. You turned heads wherever you went, without even trying! Your sparkly blue eyes and pretty cheekbones and smile made others smile back at you. You always put others before yourself and always considerably thought of the next generation. You had such empathy, showing so much compassion towards others less fortunate than you, and you worked hard to help others without grumbling. You raised your younger siblings when you were all evacuated in the war, and you were so responsible to look out for others' safety and well-being. You were an astute bargain-hunter, and taught me about haggling. I have never met anyone who could be so stubborn, which was sheer determination on your part!

Thank you for being so kind and for teaching me so much. You are forever loved, and never forgotten.

You are with God now. -xxx-

Dearest Aunty Maureen. You achieved so, so much. You were outlandish in your own time, and lived to enjoy such self-expression, style and so, so much culture.

You lived for, and cared about protecting children. You were lead of your County, for Children under Social Services. You made so, so much of a difference. You fought to support so many innocents in need, and you inherited the Darbon Determination, most definitely. You left this world, seemingly far too soon. But that did not stop your success, and your legacy lives on, to protect children in Derbyshire from harm.

You were hilarious, witty, and so stylish. You lived in style and enjoyed art and literature from various cultures; you were very well-read, highly qualified and incredibly competent in your role, as well. God bless

you, and I hope to see you all again, in Heaven one day.
Xxx

My Godfather John.

You were written about in this book, and I will always remember you, with a smile. Your children are courageous and staying strong, aided by the love in your heart you have always given them from day 1 of their lives, and are incredibly successful, talented performing artists, as you were. Thank you for your humour, including your Maltese Mafia heritage!

You are an Angel now.

Love, and God bless you xxx

Benita. My friend. You were lost so young, and left behind a son aged 11. You were loved and successful and you were let down badly by the Justice System, and the NHS as I have been, also. You are one of so many mentally ill people who died without Justice, and after my own 4 comas, and heart attack, I realise that it could happen to any one of us. I do miss you, and I wish I could've helped you more. I understand. But your son needed you. You gave up, to prove what happened to you, as the CMHT probably pretended that you were lying or delusional... as they did and some still do, with me, and so how many others must they be doing this to? In your memory, I am applying to advocate for mentally ill people, like us. Our friendship did not happen for no reason. I am sorry most, for your son.

Your parents loved you so much, and gave you so much, but possessions and money are not everything, and you were too ill to be grateful for how loved you were. You were fashionable, an NHS worker, a talented performer and intelligent. All lost on Earth, now... but you are no longer tormented or suffering anymore. You are in Heaven. I miss our shopping trips, your wittiness and energy. God bless you xxx

Finally, a big thank you to anyone who hurt me, as in *really* badly. I need not name you. Without the abuse and harm that I experienced, my writing would not have been anywhere near this, as well as the it causing me to become a nicer person to other people, to gain strength, empathy and understanding of how it is the people who are suffering moreso, are those who wish to cause others more suffering... it seems that it's all you know, but I realise now, that happy people do not hurt other people, so I hope that you get better, and I do wish you well.

I really fear for you on a personal level, as there are numerous incidents that must've been lied about to cover all of those things up... and lying about harming someone surely may have worse repercussions in the afterlife, than harming someone, telling the truth, facing up to it, and apologising. All I can really believe is that all anyone can do is warn you. It is *you*, ultimately, who has to decide to be truthful, if you want to do the correct thing- no one can make you.

God sees all (He is Omniscient). God is all powerful (He is Omnipotent), but God is all-loving; He is Benevolent - and only God's forgiveness can free us, through His Son Jesus Christ dying to save us from our sins.

I am not judging you- it is not my place to do so. I needed to let go of any resentment I held on to; for so long, because now I am; I am free.

God loves all of us. God will understand your remorse is going to be more of a reward to you than you realise. I am so sorry that you were hurting that much that you had to hurt someone that badly, and your guilt is so obvious to me now and I realise that you are ashamed of yourself, that you know you did wrong, because you are lying still, to cover it up... which means that it was not by an accident.

You didn't deserve to come to that much harm in your childhood, that you had to harm another person, just to cope with having to live with that. You were failed In a way that I cannot imagine, but I *am* so glad that I got to know you, in particular, so well.. because, you are amazingly courageous to still be here, and to do what is best for your children now, even if you didn't before. I am glad you are still in their lives, and that you are getting healthier. For them... and for yourself.

It can happen to anyone, but rarely, and for you... it must have beyond isolated you, and caused you to avoid others, to not trust them, and it cannot be easy for you to have to live the rest of your life, knowing what you are capable of doing to someone, who would never dream of doing that back to you... and having to hide it, from everybody...for the rest of your life.

She is better now, and has decided her life does not depend on whether she is believed or not, about what happened. She doesn't need you to confess, just for her to feel able to survive anymore, and is no longer living in fear of never getting Justice, because Justice will Prevail. In the Afterlife, if not in this one, and I am grateful for the love in my heart for you, and that if you are reading my warning, you realise I care about you still

 Always will.

Actions have consequences: remember this...and remember me. I will never forget you, and you gave me the three best days of my life, despite everything else. There is so much that you are capable of, and you are incredibly capable, as well as highly intelligent.

God bless you and take care.

Identity. Inclusion. Insight.

This wiill be a new chapter for me...

Printed in Great Britain
by Amazon

35935385R00081